This book belongs to

_____

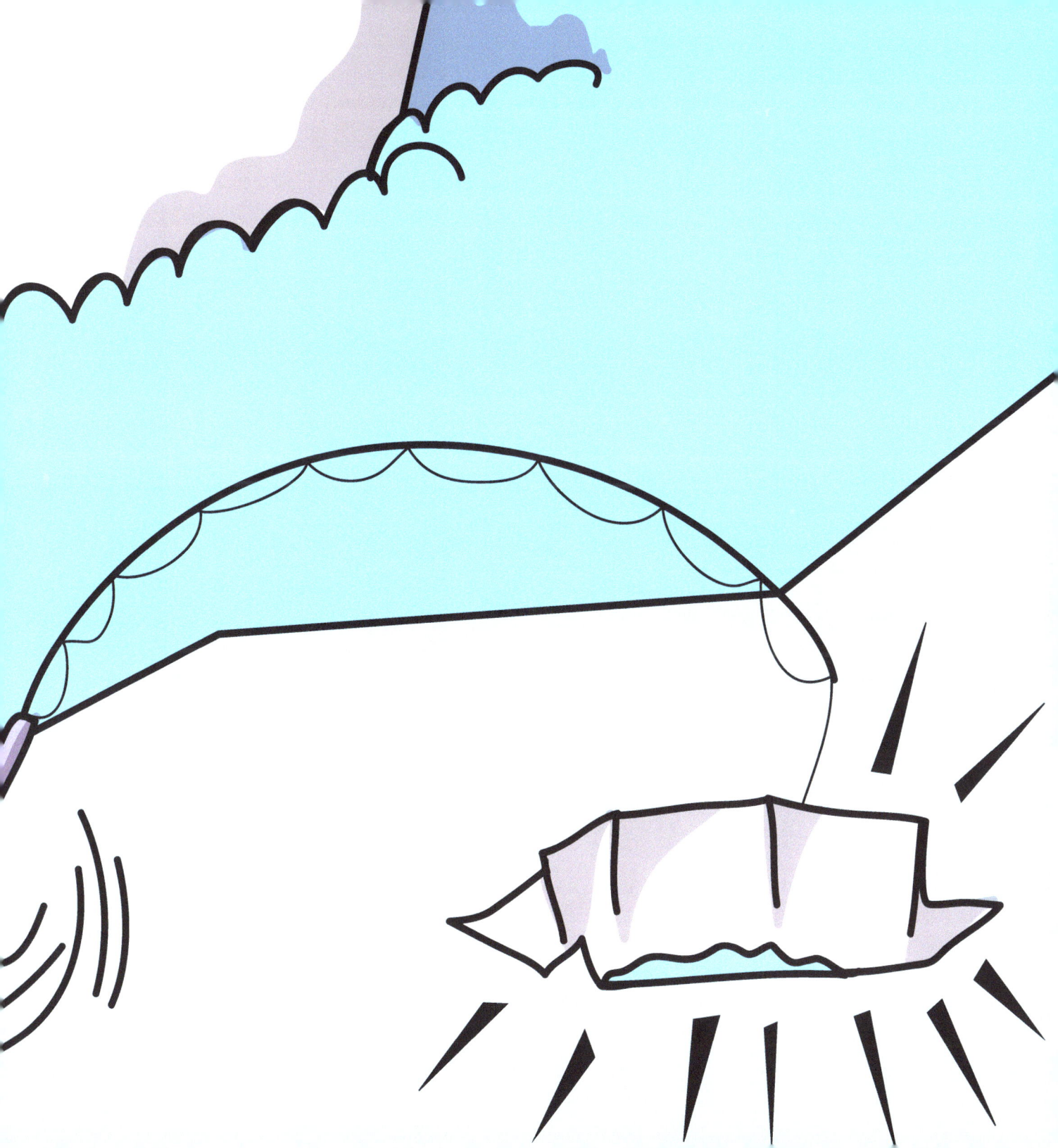

Copyright © 2025 Grow Grit Press LLC. All rights reserved. No part of this book may be reproduced in any form without permission in writing from the publisher. Please send bulk order requests to info@ninjalifehacks.tv

Paperback ISBN: 979-8-89614-097-9
Hardcover ISBN: 979-8-89614-099-3
eBook ISBN: 979-8-89614-098-6

Printed and bound in the USA.
NinjaLifeHacks.tv

Patient Penguin was always in a rush.
Her flippers flapped, her cheeks would blush.
If waiting took more than a beat,
she'd huff and puff and stomp her feet.

At lunch, in the **Social Superhero Café**,
Penguin's belly rumbled right away.
The fishy stew smelled oh-so-good,
but waiting? Penguin misunderstood.

"I'm starving! This is way too slow!
Why don't they call my name to go?"
She groaned, sighed, and crossed her wings.
With patience gone, she caused some flings.

Anxious Alpaca was next in line,
yet she stood calm with no whine.
She turned to Penguin, shook her head,
with a knowing grin, she gently said:

"Rushing won't make time move fast,
but I know a trick that's built to last.
When waiting feels too tough to do,
try the Three T's—they'll pull you through."

The Three T's

"Take three breaths: just breathe slow.
Fill your belly, let it flow.
In through your nose, out through your mouth,
Let go of the stress, release all doubt."

First T: Take Deep Breaths.

Penguin huffed, "That sounds kinda weird."
But Alpaca just grinned and gently cheered,
"Just try it once—you might just see,
a little breath can set you free."

Penguin closed her eyes and gave it a shot.
She filled her lungs, then breathed a lot.
Her shoulders dropped, her flippers light—
Hey, maybe Alpaca was kinda right.

"Next up," said Alpaca, "is what you say.
Your thoughts can shape a better day.
Instead of, 'Ugh, this isn't fair and it's so late!'
Tell yourself, 'Good things come to those who wait.'"

Second T:
Tell Yourself Good Things Come to Those Who Wait

She took a breath and stood up straight.
"Good things come to those who wait."
And oddly, as those words sunk in,
she didn't feel as mad within.

Good things come to those who wait.

"One more T left to do!
Be sure to think it through.
Before you stomp or start to whine,
Will this help or cross the line?"

Third T:
Think About the Consequences

Penguin scratched her head and thought a bit,
and pictured when she'd had a fit—
like last week at the fish fry stand,
when nothing changed from her demand.

Or last time in the movie line,
she stomped her feet and let out a whine.
She still didn't get her way,
and pouting only spoiled her day.

"So all I do is the Three T's,
and I'll feel more patient, and at ease?"

Alpaca nodded. "Yep, that's all it takes.
The Three T's fix impatient shakes!"
Penguin sighed and stood up tall and straight.
"Alright, alright—I guess I'll wait."

The stew was warm, the fish divine—
and waiting now? It felt just fine.

Next week, Penguin stood in line once more,
at the ice cream shop near the Glacier Store.
The line was long, her stomach tight,
but Penguin remembered: "I'll be alright."

She took deep breaths (one, two, three).
She told herself (good things will be).
She thought ahead (it's worth the wait).
And guess what? The treat still tasted great!

Now anytime Penguin wants things quick,
she knows the Three T's will do the trick.
Patience isn't always fun,
but with practice, it can be done.

So next time you feel stuck in line,
or waiting takes too much time,
Try the Three T's—just like Penguin—
and turn your wait into a win!

Patience isn't easy, but it sure is tasty!

Penguin's Three T's Practice

1. Take Three Breaths

What kinds of thoughts have you had today:

- Close your eyes and take three slow breaths.
- Breathe in through your nose and out through your mouth.
- Notice how your body feels: Are your shoulders looser? Do you feel calmer?

2. Tell Yourself Something Positive

- Think of a helpful phrase when you feel impatient:
  » "Good things come to those who wait!"
  » "I've got this—I can stay calm!"
- Say it out loud or quietly in your mind.

3. Think It Through

- Ask yourself, "Is stomping or whining going to help?"
- Imagine a better way to cope—like playing a quiet game or humming a silly song while you wait.

Check out the Anxious Alpaca lesson plans and more of the series at ninjalifehacks.tv

Social Superheroes

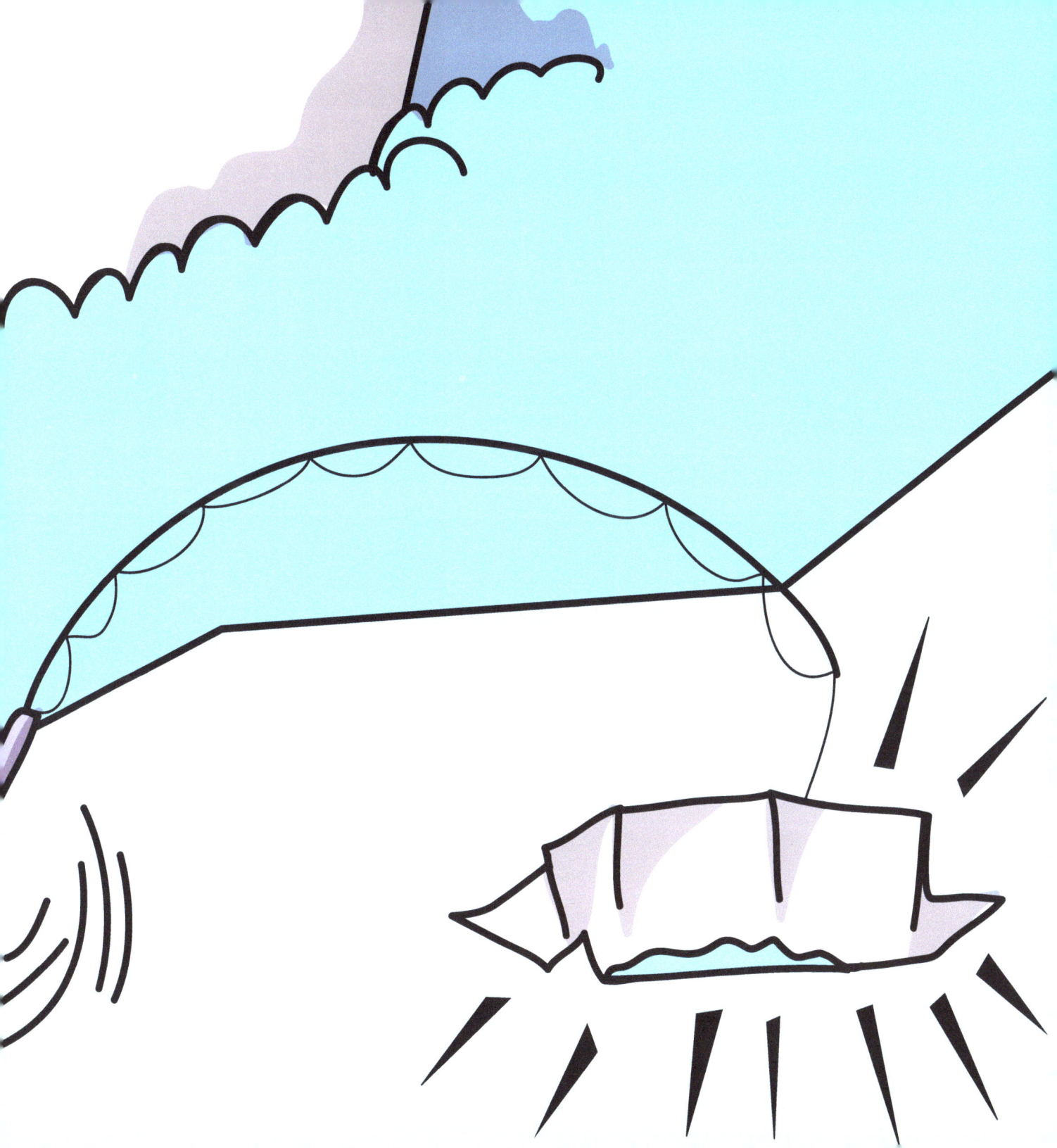

www.ingramcontent.com/pod-product-compliance
Lightning Source LLC
LaVergne TN
LVHW070436070526
838199LV00015B/522